FUN AND GAMES

COMIC CONVENTIONS

Division

COMIC CONVENTION
4-Day Pass

Kristy Stark, M.A.Ed.

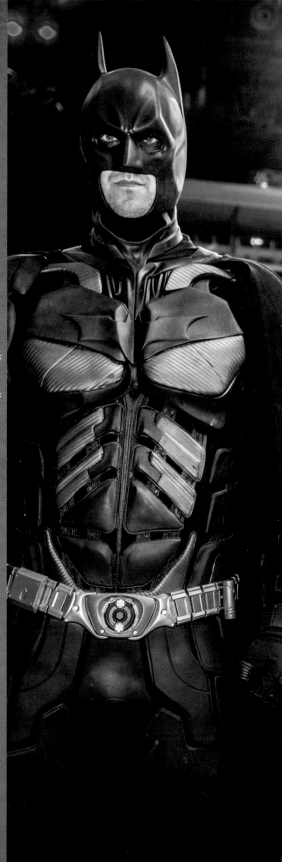

Consultants

Lisa Ellick, M.A.
Math Specialist
Norfolk Public Schools

Pamela Estrada, M.S.Ed.
Teacher
Westminster School District

Publishing Credits

Rachelle Cracchiolo, M.S.Ed., *Publisher*
Conni Medina, M.A.Ed., *Managing Editor*
Dona Herweck Rice, *Series Developer*
Emily R. Smith, M.A.Ed., *Series Developer*
Diana Kenney, M.A.Ed., NBCT, *Content Director*
Stacy Monsman, M.A., *Editor*
Kristy Stark, M.A.Ed., *Editor*
Kevin Panter, *Graphic Designer*

Image Credits: P.3 ColobusYeti/iStock; p.5 (bottom) Karl Denham/Alamy; p.8 Paul Slade/Paris Match via Getty Images; pp.9, 13 TK/Courtesy of San Diego History Center; pp.10, 29 Sam Aronov/Shutterstock; p.11 Marc Tielemans/Alamy; p.12 California California/Alamy; p.15 Roi Brooks/Alamy; p.16 Mindy Duits; p.17 (left) Boston Globe/Getty Images; p.17 (right) AFB/ZOJ/Tony Forte/WENN/Newscom; p.18 (bottom) Stephen Barnes/Alamy; p.20, 22 (top) Zuma Press/Alamy; p.23 Laurie Goldfarb/Alamy; p.24 Casey Rodgers/Invision for Stan Lee's Comikaze Expo/AP Images; p.25 (right) Lauren Elisabeth/Shutterstock; p.31 Beto Chagas/Shutterstock; all other images from iStock and/or Shutterstock.

Teacher Created Materials

5301 Oceanus Drive
Huntington Beach, CA 92649-1030
http://www.tcmpub.com

ISBN 978-1-4258-5807-0

Table of Contents

A Comic Obsession

The only thing Zach wants to do is read his comic books. He reads them while he eats breakfast. He daydreams about them while he's at recess. As soon as he gets home, he finishes his homework so he can read them while he has a snack. His mother jokes that he probably dreams about comic books, too. Even though Zach won't admit it, he actually does dream about comic book superheroes!

Zach plans to spend his entire summer vacation feeding his obsession. He'll read comic books and share them with his friends. He'll do small jobs for neighbors to earn money to buy tickets to Comic-Con®.

However, Zach's mom has different plans for his first day of summer vacation. "Mom, I just want to stay home to read my comic books!" whines Zach.

"I understand, Zach, but we are going to visit your uncle today. I haven't seen him in a long time, and he hasn't seen you since you were a baby. He's an interesting man who has lived an amazing life. I really think you will enjoy your time with him. He even knows a thing or two about comic books. You might learn something from him."

Comic books can be read in print or on digital devices.

What on Earth am I going to learn about comics from my uncle? thinks Zach. But, he figures that it is pointless to argue with his mother. At least he can read some comics in the car while they travel.

When they arrive at Uncle Graham's house a few hours later, Graham greets Zach and his mother.

Zach is very surprised to see that Uncle Graham doesn't dress as professionally as his mom does. Uncle Graham wears sneakers, jeans, and a T-shirt. The most surprising part is that he's wearing a T-shirt with a comic character that Zach recognizes: Green Lantern!

"How do you know about Green Lantern?" asks Zach.

"Green Lantern has been my favorite comic book character since I was a kid, Zach. I've loved and collected comic books since I was around 10 years old. Did you know that my father, your grandfather, even attended the very first comic book **convention**?"

"Grandpa went to the first Comic-Con? I'm saving my money so I can hopefully go one day!"

"Yes, he attended the very first one, but it wasn't in San Diego like it is today. Let me get his old photo albums to show you pictures from that first convention."

LET'S EXPLORE MATH

Zach has 75 comic books. His mom wants him to store them in boxes instead of leaving them on the floor of his room. Each box holds 12 books. How many boxes does he need? Why?

The First Comic Convention

Zach is stunned to see Grandpa Al's photos. Graham tells him that the first convention was held in New York City on July 27, 1964. He shows Zach the photos and talks about the convention.

"The first convention was called *Comicon*. There were only about 100 people, and it was held on a hot day in July. Phil Seuling (SOO-ling) brought a case of soda to help the **attendees** cool down from the heat."

Zach's blank face indicates that he has no idea who Seuling was, so Graham decides that Zach needs to learn more about the history of the conventions.

How Collectors Got Their Comics

Seuling came up with the idea to have comic **publishers** sell directly to collectors and fans. This way, fans could buy the exact comic books they wanted from the publisher. Comics were previously sold like newspapers. They were sold at stands that had a new supply each day. The comic books that were not sold that day were returned to the publisher for a refund. The publisher recycled the returned books to make more books.

Phil Seuling

Seuling thought of a way to make sure that all comic books were sold. His idea would mean more money for the publishers. It would mean more comic books in the hands of fans, too.

LET'S EXPLORE MATH

About 100 people attended the first comic convention in New York City. Now, about 180,000 tickets are sold! How many times greater is the attendance now? Choose your answer, and explain how you know it is reasonable.

- **A.** 18
- **B.** 180
- **C.** 1,800
- **D.** 18,000

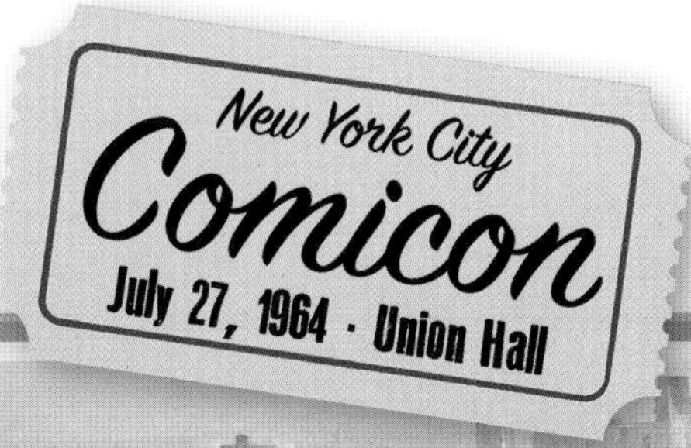
New York City
Comicon
July 27, 1964 · Union Hall

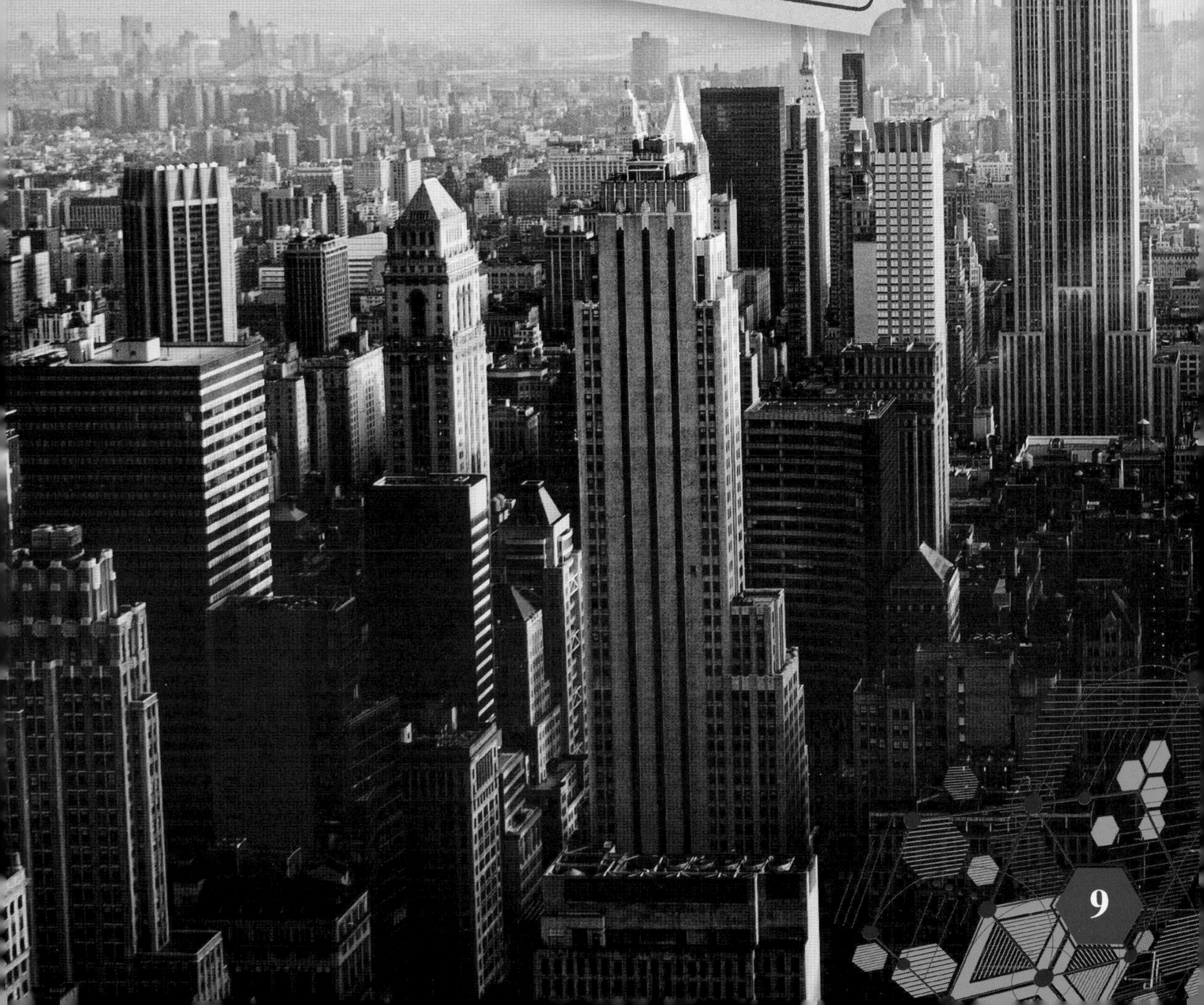

Attendees look through boxes of comic books at a convention in New York City.

Seuling set up a system for collectors to preorder comic books. Collectors would give him their money to order what they wanted. He would place an order directly with the publishers. Then, he would distribute the comics to the people who ordered them.

Seuling had a huge impact on the future of publishers, collectors, and fans. His idea changed the way publishers sold comic books. It changed the format of comic conventions, too. At future conventions, the publishers would interact with the collectors. And, they would sell comics directly to the fans.

Fans and Creators Interact

Zach states, "So I guess we have Seuling to thank for the way we buy comics."

"You're right, Zach," says Graham. "But there are lots more people that helped shape the conventions."

Graham explains how the convention was the first time that fans met the creators and artists of their favorite comic books. Bernie Bubnis planned the event. He wanted fans to interact with artists and creators. So, he invited Tom Gill to talk about how to draw comics. Gill was the artist of a comic book series called *The Lone Ranger*.

Steve Ditko attended the first convention, too. He was the artist of the original Spider-Man comic books. Ditko drew the cover art on the **program** for the 1964 convention.

1956 comic book cover drawn by Tom Gill

Comic-Con International: San Diego

Zach is **reeling** after all the info Graham shared. "Wow, I didn't know any of this!" exclaims Zach. "Can you tell me more about the San Diego convention?"

"Of course! It is now the most famous comic event. It started in San Diego, California." Graham finds the photos of that day. "It happened on March 21, 1970. It was a one-day event." He tells Zach it was called the Golden State Comic-Minicon.

The event took place at the U.S. Grant Hotel in downtown San Diego. The goal was to raise money for a larger event. The event's planners, including Shel Dorf, Ken Krueger, and Richard Alf, hoped to get fans interested in a larger comic event, too. There were about 100 people at the first event. Films and science fiction books were included.

In 1972, the event's name was changed to San Diego's West Coast Comic Convention. It was renamed San Diego Comic-Con in 1973. All the name changes did not **deter** people from attending. The number of people increased each year. In 1995, planners changed the event's name one more time. It was named Comic-Con International: San Diego (CCI). This name is still used, and fans are still flocking to attend. In recent years, the event has hosted more than 135,000 fans.

U.S. Grant Hotel

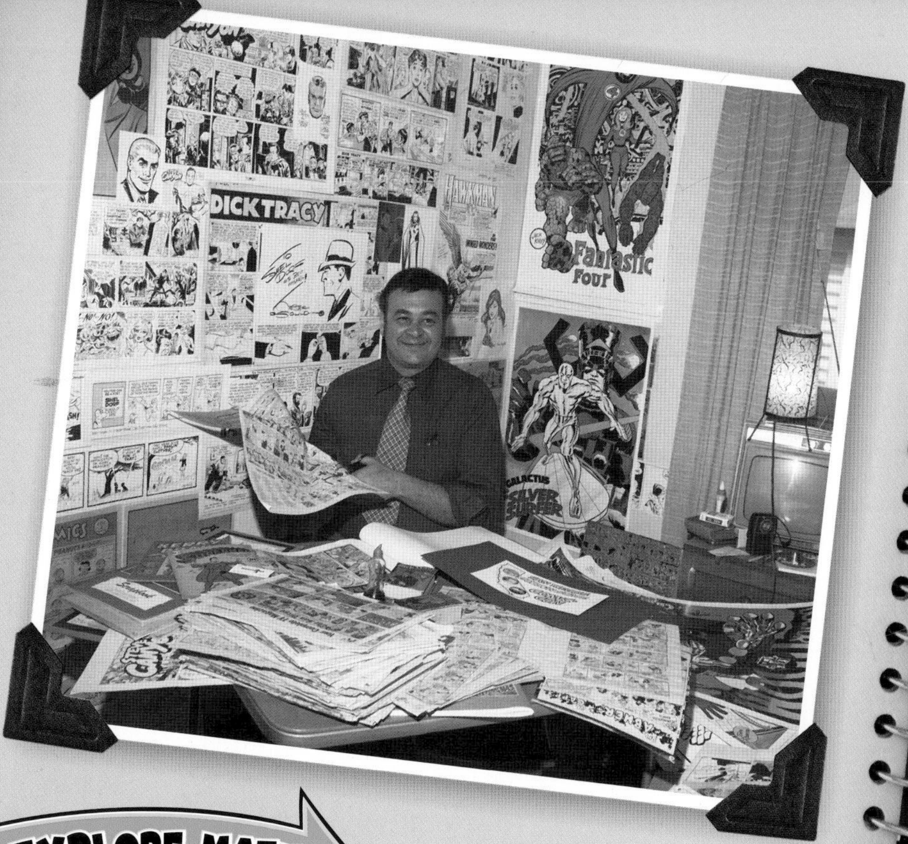
DICKTRACY
Fantastic Four
GALACTUS
SILVER SURFER

LET'S EXPLORE MATH

The exhibit hall at Comic-Con has about 42,000 square meters of floor space. There are 728 exhibitors scheduled to display booths.

1. Imagine that each exhibitor will occupy the same amount of floor space. Convention planners want to estimate this amount. Which expression should they use to make their estimate? Explain your reasoning.

   A. 42,000 ÷ 700 **B.** 42,000 ÷ 800

2. Which of the following is the best estimate for the amount of floor space each exhibitor occupies? Explain your reasoning.

   A. about 6 square meters
   B. about 60 square meters
   C. about 600 square meters
   D. about 6,000 square meters

Attending Comic-Con

Zach is so happy that he was able to spend the weekend with his uncle. He plans to see much more of him in the summer.

After Zach returns home, he gets a text message from Graham. The text reads, "I've got a BIG surprise for you—call me ASAP!" Zach dials Graham's number excitedly.

A few minutes later, Zach runs out of his bedroom to tell his mother the great news! His uncle is taking him to Comic-Con for his birthday!

That night, Zach can barely sleep.

The next morning, Uncle Graham arrives early. "Are you ready to go, Zach?"

"Yes! I've been waiting my whole life to go! I'm more than ready!" replies Zach.

When they arrive at the convention, Zach can hardly believe he is there. There are so many things to see and do. Luckily, Uncle Graham is basically a **professional** when it comes to attending the convention.

COMIC-CON INTERNATIONAL: SAN DIEGO

4-DAY PASS ATTENDEE

GOOD FOR ALL FOUR DAYS
THURSDAY-SUNDAY

NOT FOR RESALE · NO PREVIEW NIGHT · NO ADMISSION OR REGISTRATION ON ANY OTHER DAY

Comic-Con is so large that some events are held at a nearby theater instead of the convention center. Imagine that 4,000 convention-goers attend events at the theater. The theater hosts 16 events with the same number of people at each. Complete the partial products model to find out how many people attend each event at the theater.

$$
\begin{array}{r}
16\overline{)4,000} \\
-\underline{} \quad (200 \times 16) \\
800 \\
-800 \quad (\underline{} \times 16) \\
\underline{} \\
0
\end{array}
$$

Tips and Tricks

Graham has learned that with careful planning, he can see and do as much as possible. He shares his tips with his nephew, so Zach can look like a pro, too.

Graham told Zach to wear comfortable shoes. They will do a lot of walking and standing in lines. Zach is grateful that his feet won't be sore.

They bring their own snacks and water, so they are not hungry or thirsty while waiting in long lines. They don't waste time trying to find food throughout the day, and they won't have to spend extra money on snacks.

Before arriving, Graham and Zach reviewed the convention schedule and decided exactly what they wanted to do. Graham warns that it is not possible to see everything, so they figure out which events are most important to Zach.

Zach wants to attend a few **panels**. Graham recommends that they get in line at least a couple hours before the panels start. He also informs Zach that some people have to get in line five to six hours before popular panels.

A comic fan dresses as a superhero to walk around the exhibit hall.

A long line forms for a comic convention.

A convention-goer pedals his way through the convention.

Crowds explore Comic-Con's exhibit hall.

SKETCH

An artist draws sketches for fans at a comic convention in Ireland.

18

What to See and Do

There is a huge **exhibit** hall that has a variety of booths set up.

Game companies and movie studios set up displays in the hall. Publishers of comic and science fiction books set up booths, too. They have information about their new products and movies that will come out soon. They often give fans free items with the company's name or movie title. Zach and Graham are prepared with tote bags to carry all of their loot from the exhibit hall.

Visitors can spend nearly an entire day looking at all of the booths in the hall. **Vendors** sell many different things for people to buy. They sell comic books and graphic novels. Some comic collectors visit many booths to find specific books they need for their collections.

There are vendors who sell costumes and T-shirts, too. Some vendors sell collectible **replicas** of characters or items from comics and movies. People can also buy art supplies, posters, and jewelry at the booths.

Graham points out Artists' Alley in the exhibit hall. He explains that this is where artists, actors, and authors have tables set up to meet fans. Zach spends lots of time exploring this area.

Actors Will Ferrell, Tina Fey, and Jonah Hill discuss their movie, *Megamind*, at the Comic-Con press panel.

The artists, authors, and actors sign autographs for fans. Zach waits in line to have his picture taken with his favorite artist. The artist draws a quick sketch for Zach. "I'm going to keep this forever," he tells Graham.

Panels are a huge part of the convention. A panel is a small group of people who gather together to discuss a particular topic. **Industry** professionals speak at the panels. Panels give fans a chance to learn and hear about topics related to comics, games, and movies. Some actors participate in **Q&A** (question and answer) sessions. They answer fan questions and speak about their experience filming the movie. In recent years, film studios have made movies based on Marvel Comics® and DC Comics™. People want to see the actors that have portrayed their favorite comic characters. There is a huge variety of panel topics. So, there is a topic for just about everyone at Comic-Con.

An artist sketches during an exhibition.

A huge part of the convention is the costumes! Lots of fans come dressed as their favorite characters. Other fans dress like video game or TV characters.

There is a **masquerade** costume contest on Saturday evening. All participants have costumes they have made themselves. Awards are given for many categories. The contest is always a **highlight** of the weekend. Zach wants to see the contest.

"We should get in line early to get seats for the contest," explains Graham.

LET'S EXPLORE MATH

Panels are held in 19 different rooms at the convention center.

1. Imagine that there are 3,192 folding chairs for panel attendees. Each room must have the same number of chairs. Estimate the number of chairs in each room. Do you think your estimate is greater than or less than the exact answer? Why?

2. Complete the area model to find the number of chairs in each room.

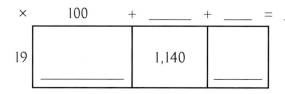

×	100	+ _____	+ ____	= _____
19	_____	1,140	_____	

A Comic-Con attendee dresses as superhero Black Canary.

More Comic Conventions

As they wait in line, Zach asks Graham if there are other comic conventions.

An Aquaman fan attends New York Comic-Con.

Graham tells Zach, "Conventions in San Diego and New York City are the most popular. They have the highest numbers of attendees. But, there are lots of comic conventions. They have costumes, artists, and fans, too." He tells Zach about other conventions as they wait in line.

New York Comic-Con® (NYCC) started in 2006. More fans than were expected showed up the first year of the event. NYCC's planners had to send away thousands of fans. They did not have enough space for them. In the years after that, planners were more prepared for large crowds. Numbers have increased each year. Around 180,000 fans now go to NYCC.

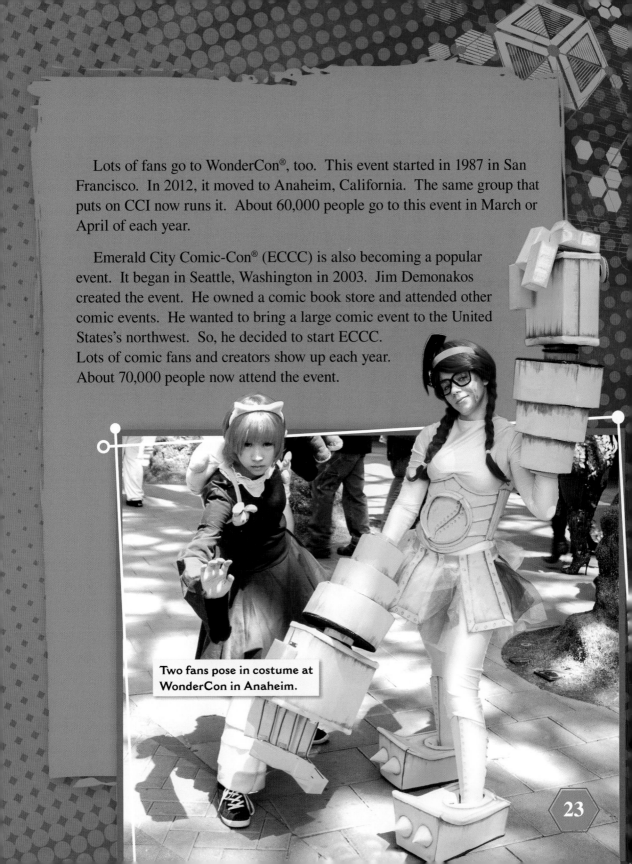

Lots of fans go to WonderCon®, too. This event started in 1987 in San Francisco. In 2012, it moved to Anaheim, California. The same group that puts on CCI now runs it. About 60,000 people go to this event in March or April of each year.

Emerald City Comic-Con® (ECCC) is also becoming a popular event. It began in Seattle, Washington in 2003. Jim Demonakos created the event. He owned a comic book store and attended other comic events. He wanted to bring a large comic event to the United States's northwest. So, he decided to start ECCC. Lots of comic fans and creators show up each year. About 70,000 people now attend the event.

Two fans pose in costume at WonderCon in Anaheim.

In 2011, Comikaze Expo® began in Los Angeles. It was modeled after CCI. Comic creator Stan Lee noticed the event. Lee is one of the most famous names in comic books. He used to be the president of Marvel Comics. During his career, he worked with artists to create Spider-Man and the Hulk. He created Iron Man, Fantastic Four, and X-Men, too.

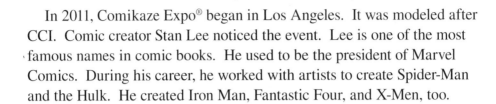

So, when Lee wanted to partner with Comikaze planners in 2012, they agreed. They even added his name to the event, calling it Stan Lee's Comikaze Expo. Then, in 2016 it was renamed again as Stan Lee's L.A. Comic Con. About 75,000 fans attend each year in October.

Stan Lee (right) welcomes fans to his Comikaze Expo with comic book artist and entrepreneur Todd McFarlane (left) in 2012.

As the name suggests, Megacon®
is a big comic event. It is held in Orlando,
Florida, every May. It is one of the largest events in
the southeastern United States. It includes comics,
sci-fi, **anime** (AH-neh-may), horror films, and
gaming. Crowds usually exceed 100,000 fans.

"For comic book lovers like us, there are so
many events to choose from!" says Graham.

"We'll have to find another event to attend
soon," says Zach.

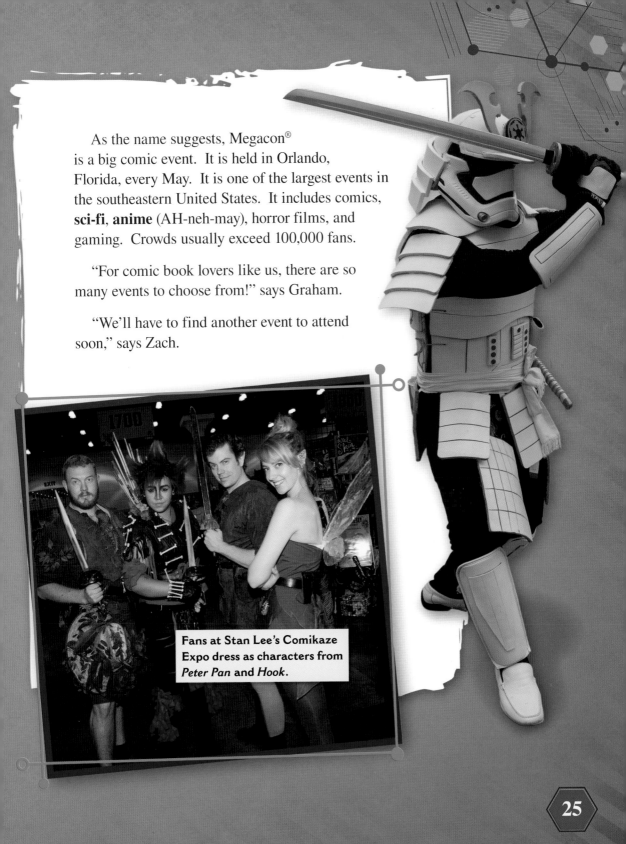

**Fans at Stan Lee's Comikaze
Expo dress as characters from
Peter Pan and *Hook*.**

Zach's experience at Comic-Con is one that he will never forget. Throughout the event, Uncle Graham taught him so many things about comic conventions and their histories.

When he gets home, Zach shows his mom photos that he took at the convention. He shows her the autographs that he collected from famous comic artists and actors, too. He tells her about everything they did and saw throughout the multi-day convention.

"What was your favorite part, Zach?" his mom asks.

"Well, I loved every part of the event, that's for sure. If I had to pick one thing, my favorite part would be spending time with Uncle Graham. He knows about comics, artists, and books. It was so much fun to hear about each convention. I will never forget this weekend as long as I live!"

"So, you won't mind visiting Uncle Graham again next month?" Mom asks.

"No, I don't mind!" responds Zach. "Seeing him will give us a chance to plan for the next comic convention we're going to in a few months."

LET'S EXPLORE MATH

After the convention, Zach reads an online news story that says hungry attendees purchased 8,160 sandwiches and salads.

1. Imagine that there were 12 snack bars at the convention center. If each snack bar sold the same number of food items, how many were sold at each location?

2. Suppose the same number of sandwiches and salads were sold at each snack bar. How many of each food item was sold?

⚙️ Problem Solving

   Comic convention attendees see the fun. But, the good times are only possible when planners pay attention to details. Convention-goers rely on planners to arrange seating for panels, organize exhibitors, order enough food, and so much more. Imagine that you are the lead planner at a convention center hosting a one-day comic convention. Prove that you understand the planning process by using the information sheet to answer the questions.

1. How much will you suggest charging attendees for tickets if the convention center needs to make $200,000 from hosting the event?

2. Each exhibitor occupies the same amount of floor space in the exhibit hall.

   a. The brochure advertising the event will only list estimates. Estimate how much floor space each exhibitor occupies.

   b. The workers setting up exhibitor booths need exact numbers. Exactly how much floor space will each exhibitor occupy?

3. You realize that not all panels can meet at the same time. How many times will each meeting room be used during the day?

4. The convention center has 2,200 folding chairs. Is this enough for all the meeting rooms to have the maximum number of seats? Why or why not?

5. There is a sold-out movie screening in the theater. The filmmaker wants to serve popcorn to everyone. The convention center's popcorn machine can make 72 servings of popcorn at a time. How many times must workers run the machine so that each moviegoer gets a serving?

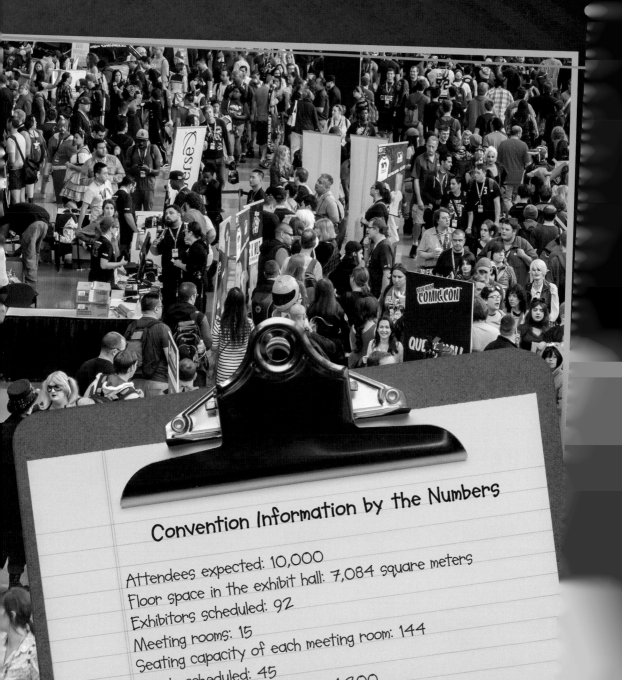

Convention Information by the Numbers

Attendees expected: 10,000
Floor space in the exhibit hall: 7,084 square meters
Exhibitors scheduled: 92
Meeting rooms: 15
Seating capacity of each meeting room: 144
Panels scheduled: 45
Seating capacity of theater: 1,200

Glossary

anime—Japanese animation

attendees—people who attend a convention, meeting, or conference

convention—a large meeting of people who share a common interest

deter—to prevent from happening

exhibit—display of objects

highlight—the best part of something

industry—a group of businesses that provide the same service

masquerade—a party where people wear masks and costumes

panels—groups of people who answer questions or give information about a subject

professional—someone who has special training, skills, or education on a particular subject

program—a small book that gives information about an event

publishers—companies that produce books, magazines, and newspapers

Q&A—question-and-answer session

reeling—feeling confused

replicas—exact or very close copies

sci-fi—short for science-fiction; imaginary stories about science

vendors—people who sell items

Index

Answer Key

Let's Explore Math

page 7:

7 boxes; 6 boxes can hold 72 books, so the 3 remaining books require an additional box.

page 9:

C; Explanations will vary but may include that $100 \times 1,800 = 180,000$.

page 13:

1. A; Explanations will vary but may include that 728 is closer to 700 than 800.

2. B; Explanations will vary but may include that $42,000 \div 700$ is 60.

page 15:

Model shows quotient of 250; 3,200; 50

page 21:

1. Estimates will vary. Example: *Each room has about 160 chairs because 3,200 ÷ 20 = 160. I think my estimate is less than the exact answer because after rounding 3,192 to the nearest hundred, I divided by 20 rooms instead of 19.*

2. Model shows quotient of 168; 1,900; 60; 8; 152

page 27:

1. 680

2. 340

Problem Solving

1. $20

2. **a.** about 70 sq. m

   b. 77 sq. m

3. 3

4. Yes; $15 \times 144 = 2,160$

5. 17 times; $1,200 \div 72 = 16$, remainder 48. Since 48 more servings are needed, the machine must be run 17 times.